First Facts™

Health Matters

Ear Infections

by Jason Glaser

Consultant:
James R. Hubbard, MD
Fellow in the American Academy of Pediatrics
Iowa Medical Society
West Des Moines, Iowa

Capstone
press®

Mankato, Minnesota

First Facts is published by Capstone Press
151 Good Counsel Drive, P.O. Box 669, Mankato, Minnesota 56002.
www.capstonepress.com

Library of Congress Cataloging-in-Publication Data
Ear infections / by Jason Glaser.
p. cm.—(First facts. Health matters)
Summary: "Describes ear infections, how and why they occur, and how to treat and prevent
them"—Provided by publisher.
Includes bibliographical references and index.
ISBN-13: 978-0-7368-6390-2 (hardcover)
ISBN-10: 0-7368-6390-7 (hardcover)
1. Otitis media in children—Juvenile literature. I. Title. II. Series.
RF225.G553 2007
618.92'0978—dc22
                                                                    2006002809

Editorial Credits:
Shari Joffe, editor; Biner Design, designer; Juliette Peters, set designer; Jo Miller, photo researcher;
    Scott Thoms, photo editor

Photo Credits:
BananaStock, 16 (main)
Capstone Press/Karon Dubke, cover (foreground), 1, 4, 8, 9, 15, 21
Corbis/Grace/zefa, 18–19; Randy Faris, 14
Getty Images Inc./Photographer's Choice/Craig van der Lende, 20
Index Stock Imagery/BSIP Agency, 7 (main)
Kevin Kavanagh, MD, 16 (inset)
PhotoEdit Inc./Michael Venture, 10–11; Robin Nelson, 13
Photo Researchers Inc./Brian Evans, 7 (bottom right); CNRI, 7 (bottom left); Eye of Science, cover
    (background)

1 2 3 4 5 6 11 10 09 08 07 06

Table of Contents

Signs of an Ear Infection

Last week, you had a cold. Now your ear hurts. It feels like something is stuck in it. Swallowing makes your ear hurt even more. It is hard to hear anything. You have the signs of an ear **infection**.

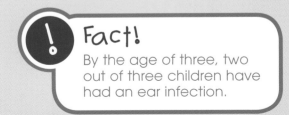

! **Fact!**
By the age of three, two out of three children have had an ear infection.

What Is an Ear Infection?

An ear infection is what happens when germs get out of control inside the ear. Normally, a tube in the ear drains fluid before germs can grow. Sometimes this tube gets blocked, trapping the fluid. Germs grow quickly in the sticky fluid. **Pus** forms and presses on the **eardrum**, causing pain.

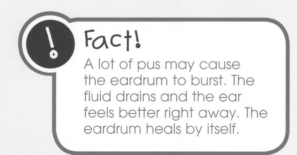

! Fact!

A lot of pus may cause the eardrum to burst. The fluid drains and the ear feels better right away. The eardrum heals by itself.

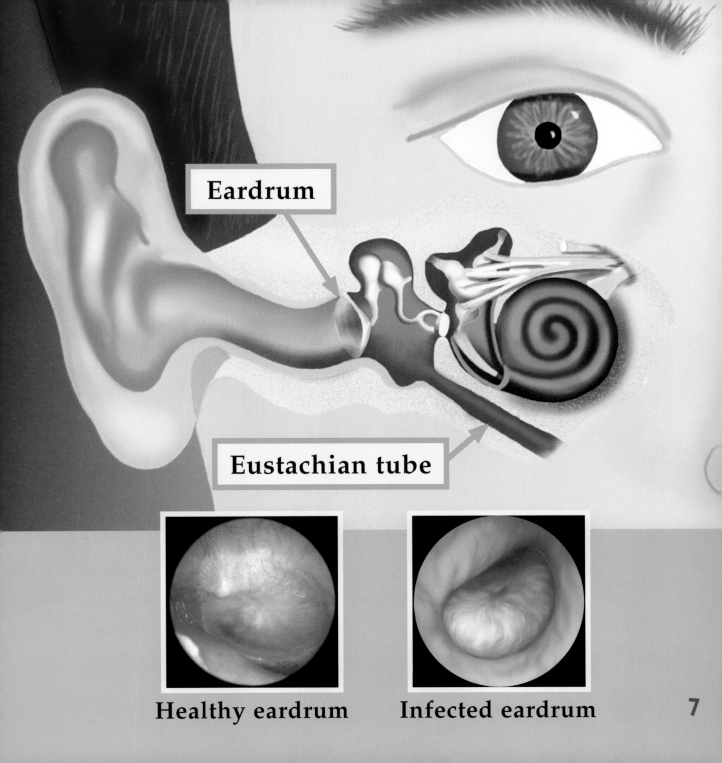

Eardrum

Eustachian tube

Healthy eardrum   Infected eardrum

How Do Kids Get Them?

Most ear infections start with a cold or flu. **Mucus** from a stuffy nose travels into the ear tube and blocks it. Fluid gets trapped, causing a middle-ear infection.

Sometimes germs and water get in
the ear while a person is swimming or
bathing. This can lead to an outer-ear
infection, or swimmer's ear.

What Else Could It Be?

Ears may hurt for other reasons. Too much earwax can block the ear and cause pain. **Allergies** also can cause ear pain and **pressure**. Even loud sounds can make your ears hurt.

People riding in airplanes feel pressure in their ears. Being up high makes the air inside your head push against your eardrums.

Should Kids See a Doctor?

Kids should see a doctor if they think they have an ear infection. Doctors use **otoscopes** to look inside the ear. Air is blown against the eardrum. If the eardrum doesn't move, the ear may be infected. The doctor will decide if medicine is needed.

Treatment

Most ear infections go away on their own. The doctor may suggest medicine just for pain. Certain ear infections may need medicine to kill the germs.

You can press a warm, wet cloth to your ear for comfort. Just don't stick anything in your ears. Poking around can make the infection worse.

16

Tube put in ear
by doctor

If It Doesn't Get Better

Sometimes an ear infection won't go away. When fluid stays in the ear for too long, it can cause hearing problems. The doctor may do simple surgery to open the eardrum and let fluid out.

Some kids get ear infections over and over. The doctor may then put a tiny tube inside the ear to help drain fluid.

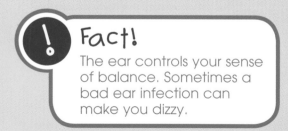

Fact!
The ear controls your sense of balance. Sometimes a bad ear infection can make you dizzy.

Staying Healthy

The best way to prevent ear infections is to not get sick. Washing hands often with soap and hot water kills most germs. Stay away from people who are sick with a cold or flu until they get better.

 Fact!
Kids often "outgrow" ear infections. As kids get older, their ear tubes get longer and can drain fluid better.

Amazing but True!

American Indians of the plains used a plant called the coneflower to fight ear infections. They also used it to treat toothaches, sore throats, coughs, and colds.

Usually the Indians mixed the plant into a tea and drank it. Sometimes they chewed the root of the plant.

Hands On:
Model Ear Infection

What You Need

clear bowl	sand
plastic wrap	radio
large rubber band	whipped cream

What You Do

1. Put plastic wrap tightly over the bowl and hold it in place with a rubber band.
2. Sprinkle a pinch of sand in the middle of the plastic.
3. Set the bowl next to the radio and turn on music with a heavy beat. Watch the sand bounce to the music.
4. Turn off the radio.
5. Remove the sand, rubber band, and plastic from the bowl.
6. Fill the bowl with whipped cream.
7. Put the plastic wrap and rubber band back on the bowl.
8. Put another pinch of sand on top of the plastic.
9. Turn on the radio. Does the sand bounce this time?

The bowl is like the middle part of your ear. The plastic is like an eardrum. Your eardrum must vibrate in order for your ear to pick up sound. The bouncing sand shows you that the plastic is vibrating. When your ear is filled with pus, like the bowl filled with whipped cream, your eardrum can't vibrate. That's why the sand probably didn't bounce when the bowl was filled with whipped cream. And that's why it's hard to hear with an ear infection.

Glossary

allergies (AL-er-jees)—reactions to things that are harmless to most people, such as foods, pets, or dust

eardrum (IHR-druhm)—a thin layer of tissue between the outer and middle parts of the ear

infection (in-FEK-shuhn)—an illness caused by germs or viruses

mucus (MYOO-kuhss)—a slimy fluid that coats the inside of a person's breathing passages

otoscope (OH-tuh-scope)—a tool used to find out if the inside of the ear is healthy

pressure (PRESH-ur)—a force that pushes on something

pus (PUHSS)—thick yellow fluid made up of cells that fight infection

Read More

Ballard, Carol. *Ears.* Body Focus. Chicago: Heinemann Library, 2003.

Glaser, Jason. *Colds.* Health Matters. Mankato, Minn.: Capstone Press, 2006.

Internet Sites

FactHound offers a safe, fun way to find Internet sites related to this book. All of the sites on FactHound have been researched by our staff.

Here's how:

1. Visit *www.facthound.com*

2. Choose your grade level.

3. Type in this book ID 0736863907 for age-appropriate sites. You may also browse subjects by clicking on letters, or by clicking on pictures and words.

4. Click on the **Fetch It** button.

FactHound will fetch the best sites for you!

Index